Enchant /
Extinguish

First published in the United Kingdom in 2021 by
Shearsman Books
P.O. Box 4239
Swindon
SN3 9FN

Shearsman Books Ltd Registered Office
30–31 St. James Place, Mangotsfield, Bristol BS16 9JB
(this address not for correspondence)

www.shearsman.com

ISBN 978-1-84861-762-9

ACKNOWLEDGEMENTS
Thanks are due to magazines where the following poems, or
earlier versions of them, were first published: *Magma* ('Buzzing'),
Poetry Salzburg Review ('In ruins', 'Trembling aspen') and *Shearsman*
('Disordered', 'After the violence', 'Archivist').

'Vertigo' was first published by the London Borough of Enfield
following a win in the Mayor of Enfield's poetry competition 2012.

Enchant /
Extinguish

M Stasiak

Shearsman Books

Contents

Buzzing

When you stretched the blanket over me
& I somehow thought of corpses
laid out in drawers in some mortuary someplace
although I was in our living room & only
almost-asleep, it held me down,
& I was a fly buzzing against steel mesh
& outside was a room & inside
was the whole of everything & I was
the mesh & the buzz as well as the fly
& the incursion into space, & when you
came to wake me gripping silent
on my shoulder on our blue settee I wouldn't
be moved, because I was a rust-spot
withering the wires & I was the crawling
through & then the buzzing free.

Vertigo

How can they tell us to
keep the music down
when crushing up around us
are the mineral sounds of industry
metal beating metal
in our ears, train-tracks driving
fractures through our bones.
How can they tell us not
to slip, when hustling
through these corridors
in sandals, trainers, desert boots
and shoes like murdered moles
a static tunnel wind
breathes vertigo.
How can they tell us
where to stand, when under
arc tubes of mercury, scandium,
thallium we could become
fluoresced and ungenerous
only skulls to store
warm chemicals inside
only eyelids to re-set us,
flickering, back through the womb.

What remains

I have been saving this weakness up all day
and now it has poured out of me
smoking in rivulets onto the stone floor.
What remains? An armature of bone.
The fish-gleam of a half-closed eye
surrendered in the skull. Coldness
drafting round the edges of the door.
Is there anything here which could be called

strength? Maybe the gravity
the insistence of this fall. Maybe
the final tired quitting of disguise.
Maybe in the recesses of flesh, inside
the cells, wrapped round the DNA,
a dark and rich hostility.

Disordered

After the edges of the world
snapped shut, and we found out
there was no *out there*
any more, nowhere to hunt
redemption or success,
we sold our neurochemistry
in cool creative ways,
and it was bad for us and we
knew it but had no strange clue
how to do otherwise,
and having taken the mammal's route,
the busy worried churning up
of soil, the fretful sore
outrunning of desire,
and rejected the reptile's
silent keeping of position
as the bad times pass,
we came out fighting,
crowded with anger and reckless
with cheap charm,
because it always was
an odd request, to see *other*
as *us,* to know the ambitious poverty
of our designs, and we are
not very good at it
not very good at all.

After we gave in to *advantage*
because everything was built on
advantage, and deification of
the way things ought to be
solidified our expectation

that there would always be *more*
always be *better*,
we realised we had no wisdom
none at all, but were only
restless for adventure,
and having confected sentiment
as truth, self-righteousness
as worth, and sought to fill
the far too fat expansion of our minds
with *busyness*,
we felt the blood-trail run
disordered in our arteries,
tangle through the black exhaust
adrenaline that's rushing in
the roadway, pausing time
and we were
not very good at looking out for ourselves
not very good at all.

After we fucked up
and refused to make apology
because the mockery was
unendurable and so was being wrong,
and bad repute began to seem
a novel and ingenious idea,
it began to dawn on us that we had no
faint notion how to play
any of it, and having feasted on
suspicion, plot, the tiny
unappeasable discrepancies
which filled us up completely
filled us up with
richness, comfort, certainty
and rage, and whispered us
against our fellows vigilant in dark,

we realised in the end
the most effective strategy
the best technique
was probably *distraction,*
and we were pleased with ourselves
because *distraction* is an infinite
enjoyable resource, and we are
good at it. Damned good.

The iron catastrophe

It was rough-cut from coal
and patterned with petrol.
It was fissured and split
and faulted from long use.
Deep beneath the surface
it was purposeful.

This is where
the core of basalt hauls
in continents, draws
them to a centre
heaving with currents
and dark resistant time.

This is where she
wakes, waits, aligns herself
against whatever happens next.
It's nothing. She is free
to acclimatise
breathe heavy patient air.

Persephone finds
a comfort in the huge
the mute, the ineluctable
begins to feel
the iron-wrangled heat
beneath the skin.

Silence reconfigures her.
They talked to you of rape?
Here there is all your fear
all of the paralysis

you visit on yourself.
Visit. Descend. And understand

how at the iron catastrophe
metal sank into itself
and came alive
atoms clenching towards their like
conspiring violent to a centre
vomiting with heat

and then extended flaring
out beyond the the night
bent back against itself
in lines of dark elaborate charge
which grip the earth
and hold their own against the sky.

In ruins

I remember cold water, the hard font,
gowns and robes, the high shadows.

I remember iron racks where I set candles
ranked in rows, threads of smoke

gone from my hand to the vaulted roof
to where promises were bound in granite.

Here still lie commandments, dice, the deadly
sins, ourselves in danger, fought for

commandeered for war among depictions
of torment, gravestones underfoot. And here

still calls a life that would be tough, take
years, endurance, take a toll in dust inhaled

words repeated over under split-glass light
where I would be viewed, valued in absolutes

and made at last to account, second
by scourged second, for everything.

Unwound from wires

The air-conditioning is not set right.
The ceiling's silver grooves are dripping
condensed breath.

                        Unwound from wires
let loose from coloured carpet tiles
a voodoo static circulates the stairs.

Sentences flop dying on my desk.
Among the plastic wood veneer I fear I could
become anything

                        squidlike, murderous.
Something struggles to comprehend in here.
Something struggles to digest.

After the corridors

After the corridors took me
        on long light-headed walks

after the mouthing of words
the edifice
        drifted loose of the world
I fled outside

I found your hide, unicorn, stripped and
        staring
left as warning on these angels
and these circuses

in a swathe of desolation
and no one saw

there is

something in us
        smooth as the table-top
shaped from the aggregate
of
        judgement

wreck

against the tarmac
strive for the just-set sun

until the broken wholeness of this
        particular night

orphans us and takes us in

After the violence

When we finally found you
six months after
the crime, the violence
you were thrown in woodland
and you were all decayed

taken in the care of those
who knew what to do with you
creatures evolved in expectation
of this mute unrushed
attention to your flesh.

Within the forest floor
they found you first
breaching the skin, the
horror, your body salvaged
in these tiny rapid lives.

It's quiet here, after
what must have been
shouting, screams.
But never think it's lonely
under the trees.

Never think you weren't
attended to, accompanied.

Trembling aspen

These are trees of disturbed land
     of displacement.
They murmur in the chained-up factory parking-lot
     after the crash
shake green and amber-gold and naked
     through the burnt-out farm
and whisper in around the shack
     abandoned
by a couple gone separately back to the city
     after that first long winter,
the 70 foot of snow to dig between kitchen door
     and unpaved road.
These are trees of transience and loss
     they listen wind-
chime fragile in the moving air
     witnessing
for one more sun-scattered lifespan
     the barn with gaping panels in its roof
the cemetery of family dogs behind the well
     recalling us
until the forest mends, memories hush,
     the conifers grow through.

The breakers

I have spent time with it and listened
to the fine-grained warm swarm
where pain and reluctance negotiate.
I have lain with it like an infection
and let it wash me through.

In the underwater swell I have
abandoned myself, become the breakers
as well as the broken upon, had faith
that sometime, if not now and if not
near to home, I will be washed ashore.

Day trip

Brendan's hand on my wrist was
hot & intense
and standing there on the walkway I declined his offer to stay

backing instead
into the steel-lined lift
retreating down through chequerboard flats, adrenaline calm

& climbing on the train with blackened eye & bleeding lip
I dumbly sat
listening to thunderstorms

while staring blankness hollowed out my chest, disconnected
eyes from face from breath, a silent
disappearing girl

& entering my own rented front door, soaking & bleak
I found Katya
– bathrobed, on her way to bed –

who said *why didn't you duck?*

Enchant/extinguish

We are landmines, we are glass
about to shatter, we are
molecules meeting in a hot
chain. We are rock heaving
beneath the surface,
eager for agency and shape.
There are more forms of disorder
than order and we go
ceaseless in search of comfort:
not there in the shaking
self-destructed night when you
concussed abandoned
left by ambulance;
not there in the sudden rage
as blade in hand you bleed
to death before a blow's
been struck; not there
in your white tight face
requesting 'a word' across
the office floor, spilling
grievance and hatred from your
inexhaustibly wronged heart.

We are landmines, we are
children warped to weaponry,
stuck juddering one
second from catastrophe.
We are Schrödinger's animals
howling and still, angels
braced and patient
in a bright collapsing sky.
The pretty altered night's
alive with chemicals

and heat; we bathe in it and
surf emotion over life-
and-death dismay, without
illusion these illusions
bring us anything but joy.
There are more forms
of disorder than order
and we are ok with that.
We have to be, held
in a spiders-web of need,
hung fragile outside safety
in a dismissive breeze.

There's no autonomy,
I don't know why
we thought there was.
Antagonised from instinct,
immobilised with artifice
and shame, we wait
inside the doorway while time
just flounders past us
order and disorder all the same.
How many lives can life
set running, enchant/
extinguish on a whim? How
many souls can pour
from heaven, seize the street,
expire like a dream?
The planet's heat beneath
turns inside out. Above it
swarms the breathlessness,
the piety, our haste, revenge;
the spinning spinning
spinning dizzy end.

Archivist

It was dusk but the sky
shone yellow
like a backwards dawn.

The crows were black on grey and
blinking, serious,
watching the first step.

And the houses turned away
as I went past.
The city shied away from me.

Understand that I was not
assassin.
I was archivist.

I came to trace your story
bring back pieces
for the tapestry, the shroud.

Behind the staggered junctions
and the grieving
streets I looked for you.

We lay inside that tiny
terraced house beside the by-pass
laughing across the dark

bound in blood and
flashing into life with lorry-lights
across the roundabout

matches striking out
discarded from your fingers
into the tin dish.

You'd have got it, this dislocated
space, this passage through
a night-time, anchored and adrift.

Streaked across the buildings
and my face
the rain blew in like judgement.

Lightning lifted up the sky
and let it drop.
I journeyed solitary, surrendered.

Far behind my back
the daylight gathers, vastly over-
whelms this restless night.

I'm left against a doorway
wrapped in grey
withdrawing into stillness.

We're diffusing, you and I,
like bruises lifting, lightening
into pale thin sky.

As the days play on

As the days play into
the distance, I will spend my
carefully gathered finance
on narcosis.
I will sip it from the bottle
uncurl my spine across the floor
and the floor will hold me with fingers
that reach inside my skin
and tether me down.

Later I will rise
and climb from my window
to a wide-boarded platform
over voided air.
I will hook my wrist
through the knotted fork of a
stripped and oiled maple branch
and feel the pull and heft of it
along my bones.

And later having died
I shall remain there
in a quiet sequence of decay –
moved as the wind
sifting through these boarded cracks
blows through my ribs as well.
And I will be the gentleness in your afternoon
the benign tick of time
above your street.

No conflagration

You have done irrevocable things.
Married your mother, for one.
Reproduced.
And now you are staked out
on the point of maximum entanglement.

Expectation crouches above your head
cuffing you into the playground,
the church, the mirrored lifts at work.
The subconscious, stabled 20 miles away
tramples and kicks.

At the end of the line

It was a good day, the day
we got them, the day we collected
the soft bright quiet rats.

Air was its proper density, settled
over stones and sea. The sea
was still and unconcerned.

Cries of the seagulls fracturing
light were random and
irreverent. The seagulls helped.

The buildings helped – unmoved,
unthinking, sprawled at rest,
crescents and terraces heaped on a hill.

The warm overcast sky helped.
The blue and white café helped, our
tea and panini next to the crazy golf.

Thoughts unwind unrealised
and the screams I heard in A&E on
Friday night disperse to space.

Leave us alone in time, beat
smooth as tumbled glass
where the train tracks stop.

Leave us to bring our animals safely
home, minding this box
of breath and beating hearts.

All of this is enough

Where do you go when you lay
on the sofa like a shot animal
wrists outstretched for the binding
eyes half-glazed, all disarranged
and nothing beautiful about you?

Back to the shack, to where no heed was paid
back to timber greyed and split.
I watched it grow lichen.
There had been animals, living and dead.
I found their skeletons among the dirt.

Where do you go at your desk
when I spot you frozen, neck
craned, staring at the street
through toughened glass
sun in your eyes, immobilised?

Into the rooms, the dim squatted rooms
adrift in the city and in my skin.
Time passed painless as water.
And there was rest and no one to judge
and outside the window cars and a dog barking.

Where do you go when kindness
disconcerts and you retreat
slow motion, beyond confusion
leaving me contained here
in our still anonymous night?

Into the centre, beyond the dense dark trees
traversing circling warmth, the ring of dawn

to watch as worlds rehearse their steps
around a clearing where there is only
and endlessly ice water running off rock.

Jens Schröter

Jesus und die Anfänge der Christologie

Methodologische und exegetische Studien zu den Ursprüngen des christlichen Glaubens

Neukirchener

Biblisch-Theologische Studien 47

Herausgegeben von
Jörg Frey, Ferdinand Hahn, Bernd Janowski,
Werner H. Schmidt und Wolfgang Schrage

Die Deutsche Bibliothek – CIP-Einheitsaufnahme

Schröter, Jens:
Jesus und die Anfänge der Christologie: methodologische und
exegetische Studien zu den Ursprüngen des christlichen Glaubens /
Jens Schröter. – Neukirchen-Vluyn: Neukirchener, 2001
  (Biblisch-Theologische Studien; 47)
  ISBN 3-7887-1877-3

© 2001
Neukirchener Verlag
Verlagsgesellschaft des Erziehungsvereins mbH
Neukirchen-Vluyn
Alle Rechte vorbehalten
Druckvorlage: Jens Schröter
Umschlaggestaltung: Hartmut Namislow
Gesamtherstellung: Breklumer Druckerei Manfred Siegel KG
Printed in Germany
ISBN 3-7887-1877-3
ISSN 0930-4800